Cleaning Shelly Beach

written by Kelly Gaffney
illustrated by Virginia Allyn

"Let's go to Shelly Beach on Sunday," said Dad.

"I don't want to go to Shelly Beach," said Nick. "We always see rubbish on the sand."

"Yes," said Mum.
"It's very sad.
It was the best beach around here."

"It can be the best beach again," said Dad.

"We can take away lots of the rubbish."

"Yes!" said Nick.

"I will ask the children at school to help, too."

Nick made a big poster.
It said ...

Please help clean up Shelly Beach.
If you can help,
come to the beach on Sunday.
From Nick and his family

The next day,
Nick put up the poster at school.
But the children did not stop to look.

On Sunday, Dad said,
"We have lots of work to do today."

"Yes," said Nick.
"It's a lot of work for one family."

"We will do the best we can," smiled Mum.

Nick and his family took lots of bags to the car. They had bags for paper, and they had bags for cans and bottles.

"Shelly Beach, here we come!" said Nick.

Dad stopped the car and they all got out.

"Look!" shouted Nick.
"My friends have come to help!"

All along the beach, lots of children had put paper, cans and bottles into boxes.

All day, Nick and his friends took rubbish away.
The clean-up took a long time.

"Thank you for helping to clean up Shelly Beach," said Nick. "It's the best beach again!"